New Beginnings

Help for New and Growing Christians

David Lowry

HopeAbides

New Beginnings
Help For New and Growing Christians
Copyright © 2013 by David Lowry

Contents

The kingdom of heaven is like a mustard seed that someone took and sowed in his field; it is the smallest of all the seeds, but when it has grown it is the greatest of shrubs and becomes a tree, so that the birds of the air come and make nests in its branches.

Matthew 13:32

1

New Beginnings

People come to God and to life in Christ in many different ways and under varying circumstances. Some are raised within a Christian community and encounter Christ within the support of a fellowship of the faithful. Others grow up in a churchly environment, sometimes more cultural than spiritual, and leave that environment when they reach adulthood. They may "rebel" or slip away, but then come back at a later time when struggles push to the forefront things heard or received in their childhood. Reminders of a possible God of love cause them to seek after God, and in seeking, find.

Others, with little experience with the Christian community beyond weddings and funerals, come into the circle of Jesus' followers through the witness of a friend. Still others come from divergent religious traditions or no religious tradition. Some count themselves as agnostics or atheists on the subject of God, before undergoing a conversion. They may enter a relatively long path which includes an intellectual grappling with the concept of God and Christian theology. They move along a path both philosophical and psychological that brings them to their personal encounter with God.

Many individuals, addicted to a chemical substance, begin a spiritual journey in a twelve step program and from there come into a Christian community. People may reach out for God in the midst of grief and loss, sickness and inner pain—some having been abused, others obsessed or oppressed, some lonely or seeking meaning and purpose for their lives. They find who they are within a Christian community where they come to begin a spiritual journey.

However the journey begins, it is a spiritual one. With all the diversity of ways that people come to know Christ, they are all on a spiritual journey. That journey, with its varied experiences among different individuals, has common contours. We can talk about a shared experience—the experience of God's work in our lives. If you have come into this "new life" and are beginning to learn the terrain this journey takes you through, and you would like some guide posts and a map for the journey, this book is for you.

The new life that comes from God is like the smallest of seeds that grows and "becomes a tree, so that the birds of the air come and make nests in its branches" (Matthew 13:32). It starts small and grows into a reality that supports and nurtures life. It begins, perhaps, with a word or a thought from God. We may not know, at first, that it is from God, but like a small seed, it falls on the fertile soil of an open, needy heart. It tugs at the heart, calling for a response: "Come to me, all you that are weary and are carrying heavy burdens, and I will give you rest."

We become engaged with something God is doing in us. Some of us simply welcome what God is doing. We are like thirsty people in a desert who find water. There is nothing that stops us from drinking. We do not struggle over whether this is the water we really want. We have no where else to go. There was a time in Jesus' ministry when people were leaving Jesus because his words were too hard, and he turned to his twelve disciples and said, "Do you also wish to go away?", to which Peter replied, "Lord, to whom can we go? You have the words of eternal life" (John 6:68).

Like Peter, we have come to realize that we have no where else to turn. Without God our lives are meaningless, and we are weighed down by guilt, or we have been crushed by pasts hurts—the sins of others against us, or we are in bondage to some addiction or obsession that is playing havoc with our lives. We have no place to turn until we hear a word or message from God that truly addresses us. We desperately need the word, and welcome it and the new life that it brings.

For many of us, welcoming the new life is not immediate. We struggle. We do not easily come to God. We are like Augustine, the fifth century bishop of Hippo in northern Africa. In his *Confessions*, he shares his struggle with becoming a Christian. He tells us he was attracted to the new life that he saw among Christians. He kept going to hear a preacher named Ambrose. He was drawn to the message. He thought about getting baptized, but kept putting it off because he realized it would mean giving up his mistresses. Finally, he heard news of a prayer movement in northern Africa where he was from. There were people going out into the desert to pray for the world. They were leaving behind everything. He realized how great Christ must be for people to leave everything for him. This new life was like the pearl of great price that Jesus said a person will sell everything for in order to have. Augustine started to wrestle in prayer.

He was amazed at how greatly his will was in bondage. He wanted what Christ offered but could not choose. He found himself in a great tug of war. He had thoughts that began to focus on those mistresses. " They tugged at my fleshly garments and softly whispered: 'Are you going to part with us? And from that moment will we never be with you any more? And from that moment will not this and that be forbidden you forever?"' Augustine found himself torn between his desire to be rescued and the desires of the flesh. He described it like this: "The enemy held my will; and of it he made a chain and bound me. Because my will was perverse, it changed to lust, and lust yielded to became habit, and habit not resisted became necessity. These were like links hanging one on another—which is why I have called it a chain—and their hard bondage held me bound hand and foot" (Augustine, *Confessions*). When he finally "let go" and turned his life over to God, he knew it was by God's grace. The small seed of "God's kingdom," (to use Jesus' words) took root and sprouted. God began to reign in Augustine's heart and over his desires.

God does this for each of us who come to him. God draws us to himself and helps us to believe and receive. The seed takes root and begins to grow. Eventually, a fresh seedling of new life comes forth. What was sown in the depths of our hearts now manifests itself in the experience of being welcomed by God. God is merciful and forgiving. We may find ourselves experiencing joy and peace, changed desires, new-found purpose and new perspectives. We are starting to see things differently—ourselves and others. The new life sown has taken root, sent forth shoots and is beginning to blossom. We find ourselves crying out to God in personal terms, "My father, my mother," as we experience God's nearness. ("When we cry, 'Abba! Father!' it is that very Spirit bearing witness with our spirit that we are children of God" (Romans 8:15).

We feel ourselves to be "babes in Christ." We want to grow as children of God. We want God to keep speaking to us, revealing more to us of what he has for us and what he is doing in our lives. At the same time, however, this new life is having to grow in a hostile environment, in the midst of self-deception, misdirected desires, hurts, bitterness, selfishness and unbelief. It is not a very healthy place for a newborn. It is a place of confusion: "I do not understand my own actions. For I do not do what I want, but I do the very thing I hate. Now if I do what I do not want, I agree that the law is good. But in fact it is no longer I that do it, but sin that dwells within me. For I know that nothing good dwells within me, that is, in my flesh. I can will what is right, but I cannot do it. For I do not do the good I want, but the evil I do not want is what I do. Now if I do what I do not want, it is no longer I that do it, but sin that dwells within me" (Romans 7:15-17).

We reach out for forgiveness and cleansing, and it is there for us: "If we confess our sins, he who is faithful and just will forgive us our sins and cleanse us from all unrighteousness" (1 John 1:9).

We may wish that this new life would grow faster and take over the unruliness of our hearts. But we need more of *God's Word* (God speaking to us personally) and *God's Spirit* (God's power and presence) for this new life to grow. We are finding that we must keep feeding this new life. We need to keep seeking and listening for God's messages to us. We have spent years filling our hearts with false messages and now we need truth. We need God to speak to us, and with every word that comes from God (God has ways of getting through to us), we find we have to turn from what is false and trust in what God is telling us.

The notion of "God telling us" something, is new. We may not be used to thinking or talking about God speaking to us. And yet, it is part of the language of the Bible and other

Christians. It is a way of recognizing that the truth that is finally getting through to us about ourselves is coming from God. Gods' Spirit is at work in us. The "eyes of our hearts" are being enlightened. And God has more of that reality for us. There are times when we are reading the Bible and understanding little, and then, all of a sudden, we are reading and not only understanding but realizing that what we are reading is *for us*. God is speaking to us through these words.

God addresses us through Scripture, through others, through a sermon, through nature, through circumstances and within ourselves while we are actively engaged in life's struggles and while we are in prayer. We discover prayer is not simply shooting requests "up" to God, but is a conversation with God. God has something to say to us!

God speaks to us about ourselves. God speaks to us both about our condition and about what we are becoming as children of God. We should not be surprised that, as we are open to God's Spirit working in our lives, we see things about ourselves that we have not wanted to see. We have been in denial about our true condition. We have been afraid to admit how wrong our thinking and acting has been. We have tended to put a pretty face on our actions and motivations. We have not only tried to fix up our behavior before others, but lied to ourselves about what we do and what motivates us. We have needed the Spirit of truth to help us tell the truth about ourselves.

The Holy Spirit helps us to know our condition. Jesus says he sends the Spirit to do this. "When [the Advocate or Spirit] comes, he will prove the world wrong about sin" (John 16:8). Our condition and the world's is worse than we have been telling ourselves. By the Spirit, we are now coming clean about our jealousy, covetousness, envy, selfishness, lust, sexual immorality, greed, idolatry, gossip, slander, contentiousness and overall evil ways. At first, there are things we recognize as glaringly wrong and which we must now turn away from. As our consciences are made alive, we increasingly see more. We see that it is not only what we have done that is a problem, but what we have left undone. We have not loved as we ought. When we had the opportunity, we did not love a person in need in a practical way. And it is not only our deeds that need to change, but our words and thoughts and motives as well. We have not loved God with our whole heart and we have not loved our neighbor as ourselves. "'You shall love the Lord your God with all your heart, and with all your soul, and with all your mind.' This is the greatest and first commandment. And a second is like it: 'You shall love your neighbor as yourself'" (Matthew 22:37-39).

The Holy Spirit helps us to grow in recognizing our true condition, not so that we feel accused, incriminated and condemned, but so that we are deepened in the truth and in our need for God our savior. When I go to the doctor, I want the doctor to give me a true diagnosis of my condition and the treatment that corresponds to it. I am grateful that the Spirit of God is the Spirit of truth. I need the truth. It is important that we do not fight this work of the Spirit, but learn to embrace it, not fighting against conscience, but turning daily to God for strength to overcome temptation, and walk in the way God is setting before us.

The Holy Spirit not only reveals to us our brokenness, but brings light to what we are becoming. "When the Spirit of truth comes, he will guide you into all the truth; for he will not speak on his own, but will speak whatever he hears, and he will declare to you the things that are to come" (John 16:13). The Spirit shows us what we are becoming. We begin to recognize what God is doing in our lives and where God is leading us. We deepen in our sense of who we are becoming as new creations of God. "So if anyone is in Christ, there is a new creation: everything old has passed away; see, everything has become new" (2 Corinthians 5:17)!

This "new beginning" is leading us into new living. We have much to look forward to.

No one puts new wine into old wineskins; otherwise, the wine will burst the skins, and the wine is lost, and so are the skins; but one puts new wine into fresh wineskins.

Mark 2:22

2

New Patterns

With the new life comes new patterns for living. We become seekers after God, receivers of his good gifts, obedient to his will, and grateful worshipers. The old patterns were similar except that they were not directed to God. We were seekers after the good life as defined by our desires. Our tendency was to worship ourselves and our whims, desires, attitudes and agendas.

Now our seeking, believing, receiving, repenting, obeying, thanking and worshiping has begun to be directed to God. We can be quite intentional and committed about these patterns for new life. The Holy Spirit helps us with our commitment. Our growth in the new life needs these patterns as daily habits.

Seeking

Seeking got us to the door that opens to new life. We were seeking after God before we even knew who or what to believe and even before we knew it was God we were seeking. We sought because we were troubled. Perhaps life had become so painful that we turned from that which we usually sought after to reach out to what we could not yet name. Like an alcoholic, who tells himself that he doesn't have a drinking problem, we told ourselves we were getting by okay until, like the alcoholic, we could no longer live with the breakdown in our lives. Then we started seeking.

Some of us started seeking simply because we wanted more out of life. We started realizing that there had to be more to living than simply surviving. If we heard Jesus' words, they gave us hope: "Ask, and it will be given you; search, and you will find; knock, and the door will be opened for you" (Matthew 7:7). What helped us to come to God, now also helps us to go further and deeper into the presence of God. Seeking must become a daily pattern of our lives.

Seek after God. Seek after a word from God. Seek to hear his still small voice. Seek to know God's will in order to do it. Seek the power and guidance of God's Spirit.

Seeking becomes increasingly focused as we gain understanding of the new life in Christ. We read in Romans chapter six that we are united to Christ through baptism and that we are united to his dying and rising so that we may die to the old life and rise to the new life, alive to God and his purposes for us. Therefore, we seek after Christ in order to die and rise with him daily. We stretch out for what God wants to do in our lives. Paul writes of his own seeking as a Christian when he writes, "This one thing I do: forgetting what lies behind and straining forward to what lies ahead, I press on toward the goal for the prize of the heavenly call of God in Christ Jesus" (Philippians 3:13-14). We realize that our lives are coming down to one thing: To seek and stretch out to God for what he has and how he wants to use us in this world and among the people he places in our lives.

Believing

"The life I now live in the flesh I live by faith in the Son of God, who loved me and gave himself for me" (Galatians 2:20).

Living by faith is now to become a pattern of our lives. As Paul says, "We walk by faith, not by sight" (2 Corinthians 5:7). We are to live by trusting in God and what he has done for us through Jesus Christ. Our circumstances and situations—what we see—are not to determine the steps we take, but God who leads us by his word and Spirit. We came to Christ by faith. The new life flows from faith. We grow to maturity as we walk by faith.

Believing in God is not the same as positive thinking. It is certainly not wishful thinking. We do not live in denial of the negatives in life, but persist through struggles, hurts, grief, guilt and sin, because we focus on the guidance and power of God.

By faith, we live by God's word. By faith, God's word is living and active, addressing us personally every day. By faith, we know God is present and watches over us and keeps us. By faith, we live by God's power.

By faith, we learn to exercise authority, in Christ's name, over obstacles and forces that used to overpower us. We learn to say to negative thoughts that do not come from God, "Depart from me in the name of Jesus. I am not listening to you today." We learn to take command of our desires and lusts. We tell them to sit down. By faith, we learn to take responsibility for our calling. We have a purpose today that God gives us, and we are learning to be attentive to it and live it.

Jesus is our example of what it means to walk by faith. When Jesus encountered disease and bondage, he healed and delivered. In one situation, a man brought his son to Jesus' disciples for them to heal. They were, after all, ministers in training. Jesus had given them authority to do the work of ministry that he was doing. But they failed in this instance, which was a great disappointment to Jesus. He shared with them his frustration, "You faithless and perverse generation, how much longer must I be with you? How much longer must I put up with you? Bring him here to me" (Matthew 17:17). Jesus than healed the boy by casting out a demon. His disciples later asked Jesus why they could not cast out the demon. Jesus made it clear that it was a matter of faith. "Because of your little faith. For truly I tell you, if you have faith the size of a mustard seed, you will say to this mountain, 'Move from here to there,' and it will move; and nothing will be impossible for you" (Matthew 17:20).

By trusting in God, as Jesus did, great things can be done in and through us. The good news is that this faith is available to us today through Jesus who did for us what we have been unable to do—he believed God. He operated by faith in his Father in heaven. He believed in the power of God available to him and acted in that power. He clearly wants us to operate in that power as well—by faith.

There is another way we see Jesus living by faith, and that is in how he relates to people in positions of power. He makes it clear that his desire is to do what pleases his Father, not people. To King Herod who was threatening to kill him, Jesus said, "Go and tell that fox for me, 'Listen, I am casting out demons and performing cures today and tomorrow, and on the third day I finish my work. Yet today, tomorrow, and the next day I must be on my way, because it is impossible for a prophet to be killed outside of Jerusalem"' (Luke 13:32). As far as Jesus was concerned, Herod could go on with his conspiring and his threats. It mattered little to Jesus. He was not going to give him the time of day. He had a calling and a mission, and he was committed to seeing it through. Never mind what others were thinking and doing in relation to him, he was trusting in his Father, to do his Father's will. Faith keeps its focus on God and his will. It will not be side-tracked by the strategies of others. By faith, we press on with what God is leading us to do, despite what others may think.

Faith takes on the negatives in life. In the midst of things that we do not understand, by faith we lay hold of God and his word. Jesus is our help in this. He kept trusting in his Father in heaven even in the face of rejection and death. He trusted his life to God. From the cross, he prayed, "Father, into your hands I commend my spirit." He did that for us, and is now the author and finisher of our faith. Through him faith has become possible for us.

Therefore, we must now lay aside everything that does not come from God and run the race that is set before us because Jesus is the "pioneer and perfecter of our faith." In him, we have come to believe and through him we continue to believe. Keep on believing. If you are having a difficult time believing, ask God to help you, and he will. Make it a pattern for life.

Receiving

Some, after reading about walking by faith, may be thinking, "That is too much for me. I have so little faith, and I get side-tracked so easily." Take heart, we can receive more faith. "The apostles said to the Lord, 'Increase our faith'"'

(Luke 17:5)! Faith can be increased by receiving the word, as Paul tells us: "Faith comes from what is heard, and what is heard comes through the word of Christ" (Romans 10:17). In response to their plea for more faith, Jesus spoke a word of encouragement: "If you had faith the size of a mustard seed, you could say to this mulberry tree, 'Be uprooted and planted in the sea,' and it would obey you" (Luke 17:6). With this word, Jesus was encouraging the increase of faith. There is a qualitative difference between no faith and little faith. With no faith there is no power of God. With little faith, even the size of a tiny seed, there is great power available.

In receiving that word, Jesus' apostles were experiencing an increase in faith. They were being told that the little faith they had, connected them to God's great power. It is good to be on the receiving end of God's word. Receiving what God is giving must become a pattern of our lives. "Every generous act of giving, with every perfect gift, is from above, coming down from the Father of lights, with whom there is no variation or shadow due to change" (James 1:17).

Needy people come to God to receive. The apostles needed more faith, and they came to Jesus. We are in need of what God is giving. We need more faith, more love, more hope, more power. God wants us to come to him to receive what he is giving—especially for receiving the "word of Christ," the good news of God's presence and power with us. We need to be hearers of the word, readers of the word and doers of the word. If we only hear and do not do, we do not truly receive the word.

We seek in order to receive, but sometimes our search brings us to a gift God is giving that we hesitate to take. Sometimes we realize the Lord is speaking to us about an idol in our lives, something we have been depending on, or a habit or pattern that we have told ourselves we cannot live without. God is revealing to us that what we are depending on or involved in, is not from him, and he is calling us from it to himself. We find a resistance to what God is saying to us. The resistance even manifests itself in rationalization. In various ways, we argue within ourselves that our false dependence or habit is not that bad. We give ourselves reasons why it is okay. It is actually an argument we are having with God. As long as we continue to reach out to God and open ourselves to him, the message he has for us persists. It does not go away until we receive what our Lord is saying to us by turning away from what does not belong to him and giving ourselves whole-heartily to him again.

There are many times when receiving the good gifts that God has for us happens as we turn from our resistance and rebellion to God, to again trust him. Receiving must become a pattern in our lives. It is a pattern for growth. We must learn to turn quickly from our resistance and receive what God is giving, that we may not get in the way of our growth in him. Obeying God must become a pattern of our daily living.

Repenting

Jesus came proclaiming, "Repent and have faith for the reign of God is at hand." Repentance and faith are like two sides of the same coin. We cannot have one without the other. "Repent" means to turn around or turn away from that which we have been doing or thinking in order to now receive God's reign and what he is doing. The New Testament Greek word is *metanoia* which means "change your mind." It is time to change our minds. We have been thinking one way. Now we must think differently. We had been thinking that God and his kingdom were far from us and had little affect on our lives. Now we must change our minds and know that God's kingdom is near. And we have to make up our minds about God's kingdom in order to receive it and be changed by it. It is time to turn from what we have placed our trust in and now trust our lives to God and place ourselves under God's reign.

Repentance involves, as Paul puts it, turning "to God from idols, to serve a living and true God" (1 Thessalonians 1:9). We come to Christ through the door of repentance. We grow in the new life that is ours in Christ through repentance. Daily we have opportunities to turn from ways we have been thinking or acting that are not "of Christ." We have patterns and habits of living that we did not receive from God, but from ourselves trying to play god. We have lived like we reigned, and our desires and lusts and attitudes directed our lives. We have created many idols for ourselves—images of ourselves that we have come to depend on. We have depended on ourselves to make things right, to set up life according to our own imaginations, to get people's acceptance, to have prestige or status, to be in control, and to call the shots. Now, we must daily turn our lives over to God who truly reigns and trust in the guidance and empowering of his Spirit.

Repentance must become a pattern of our lives. The Holy Spirit will keep showing us habits that we must turn from, ways of thinking that are not healthy, ways of relating to others in our lives that must change. We must now learn to keep changing our minds, keep turning from things that we used to think were okay but now know do not come from God in whom we now live and find our true being.

Make repentance a pattern for daily living. Turn away quickly from what God is revealing to you is not of him. Turn quickly to him to live by faith, obeying the promptings of God's Spirit, being open to what he is saying. Obedience to God is an integral part of repentance and another new pattern for our lives.

Obeying

Paul reminds us that we "were dead through the trespasses and sins in which we once lived, following the course of this world, following the ruler of the power of the air, the spirit that is now at work among those who are disobedient" (Ephesians 2:1-2). We have lived in disobedience to our Creator. We have run far from God and from our true selves made in the image of God. We have been in rebellion. That is the way Scripture describes us. But Paul also tells us that "God, who is rich in mercy" saved us through Christ who was raised for us that we might also be raised with him out of a life of disobedience and rebellion (Ephesians 2:4-7).

Because God has now raised us out of a life of disobedience to God, obedience is now a pattern for the new life. As more is revealed, as we hear what God intends for us, as we hear his word to us, we are to respond by obeying the word we receive from him. As with faith and repentance, so faith and obedience are like two sides of the same coin. They go together. God wants us to trust him enough to obey him.

There are many temptations we face daily. In all these temptations, we are tempted not to believe God but to trust in ourselves instead. We are tempted to rationalize our actions, to justify sins even before we commit them. Like Eve, in the story of temptation, we are tempted by the thought, "Did God really say?" and by the thought that this action that we are contemplating will be good for us even though we know, deep down, that God has revealed to us something different. The answer to such temptations is to believe God (and the promptings of his Spirit) enough to obey him.

Be quick to obey. Do not get into a mental argument over the temptation. Simply obey what the Spirit of God is revealing. Make obedience to God a pattern of daily life. This is a new pattern for the new life that is ours in Christ.

Worshiping

"The hour is coming, and is now here, when the true worshipers will worship the Father in spirit and truth, for the Father seeks such as these to worship him" (John 4:23). Worship goes to the heart of our relationship with God. In fact, whatever we worship is our god—whether money, power, pleasure or the true and living God. What our hearts bow down and submit to is our god or idol. Jesus is tempted by the devil to bow down and worship him. His answer was, "Away with you, Satan! for it is written, 'Worship the Lord your God, and serve only him'" (Matthew 4:10).

Worship is the central pattern of the new life. It includes, within it, faith, hope and love directed to God. And it involves praise and thanksgiving. I am going to focus on the praise and thanksgiving. These are extremely important patterns of the new life.

At one point in Jesus' ministry he was approached by ten lepers who desired to be healed. Jesus told them to go to the priests who would examine them to determine whether they were healed. This examination had to be done before they could enter back into the community. Jesus sent them on their way *before* healing them. On the way to the priests, they were healed. We see, in this story, the patterns of seeking, believing and obeying as well as praise and thanksgiving. These ten lepers sought Jesus out; they believed his word that sent them to the priests—even though they were not yet healed. They believed enough to obey. One of the lepers, upon being healed, turned back to give praise and thanks:

> Then one of them, when he saw that he was healed, turned back, praising God with a loud voice. He prostrated himself at Jesus' feet and thanked him. And he was a Samaritan. Then

> Jesus asked, "Were not ten made clean? But the
> other nine, where are they? Was none of them
> found to return and give praise to God except
> this foreigner?" Then he said to him, "Get up
> and go on your way; your faith has made you
> well." (Luke 17:15-19)

God wants to make us whole. He has healing for every
area of our lives, not just the area that first got us to him.
There is healing for us as we enter into worship through
praise and thanksgiving.

Notice three things about this leper who returned: He
praised God with a loud voice, prostrated himself at Jesus'
feet and thanked him. We see three elements to his worship
and ours:

1. Worship involves praising God with abandon. Just as
   the leper who praised God with a loud voice, when
   we praise God with abandon, we no longer care what
   others think. Our focus on surroundings and others
   moves to a centering in God. We are yielding and
   letting go. There is wholeness in such worship.

   Our fundamental problem is that we spend our
   days concentrating on ourselves and how we are going to fix things. In praise, we now abandon ourselves
   to God and to who he is and what he does. It is no
   longer about us.

2. Praise involves bowing our hearts to the Lord. The
   healed man threw himself down at Jesus' feet and
   lay there before him. He surrendered himself. He
   was completely bowed. He could not get any further
   down. Jesus is now his Lord. Such praise prepares
   us for hearing God speak to us. When we truly bow
   down before Jesus, we place ourselves in a position
   to hear his word and obey him.

3. Praise involves giving thanks. Thanking clears away complaining. Complaining tends to close off God's blessing. It tends toward unbelief. As long as we are saying, "Everything is a mess; things are messed up without end—forever and ever; there is nothing that can be done," we are not seeking and believing.

Thanking our Lord helps us to keep seeking and believing. When I am thanking him, I am expecting more of his good gifts. That is why it is important, as Paul says, to "thank God in all circumstances"—in the midst of the bad and the good. Thanking God changes our perspective on our circumstances. As we thank God, we are reminding ourselves that our lives and our circumstances are in God's hands. Every good and perfect gift comes from God, and he gives to us what we need when we are going through difficulties. We can keep thanking God while we are going through trials, and be open to receive from him. He is with us to deliver us.

God calls us into a pattern of life that includes seeking, believing, receiving, repenting, obeying and praising God. Do you want to experience more of God's blessing and presence? Then take on this life-giving pattern. Turn from the old patterns for the new. It is not a matter of us doing everything right or getting it all perfect or getting our lives entirely together. Rather, it is now a matter of entering into these new patterns for living, so that they become a way of life. Make it a pattern, for your life, to praise and thank God, yielding yourself to him and thanking him in all circumstances.

Fight the good fight of the faith.
1 Timothy 6:12

3

New Battles

We are familiar with the old battles. They are battles of flesh and blood. We contend with this or that person. We argue and fight over perceived slights as well as clear wrongs. We have been mistreated so we attempt to "get back." Or, we fight over what we perceive as belonging to us and our domain. We do battle over turf. What is ours, is ours. Sometimes the fight is over what we think should be ours. We envy what someone else has; we covet it. And so we do battle. We contend for position, for status, for acceptance, for acknowledgment, for control. Soap operas are filled with such battles.

We are also familiar with the weapons used: backstabbing, slander, manipulation of situations and the truth, deceit, self-righteousness, blaming and judging. Words are summoned for their potential to cause hurt—or a knife or gun is reached for. These battles are meant to inflict pain. They become vicious cycles of hurt and confusion. These are the battles of the old life.

Paul writes of a different kind of battle that comes with our new life in Christ. Do not be surprised by this battle, or fearful of it. "For our struggle is not against enemies of blood and flesh, but against the rulers, against the authorities, against the cosmic powers of this present darkness, against the spiritual forces of evil in the heavenly places" (Ephesians 6:12). The real battle is spiritual, and it must be waged with spiritual weapons.

The battle is not only against cosmic forces of evil (which, in the New Testament, are also called evil spirits, unclean spirits, demons and the devil), but against what Paul calls the flesh. "Live by the Spirit, I say, and do not gratify the desires of the flesh. For what the flesh desires is opposed to the Spirit, and what the Spirit desires is opposed to the flesh; for these are opposed to each other, to prevent you from doing what you want" (Galatians 5:16-17). By *flesh* Paul is referring to that condition we have from the old life that pridefully tries to live by its own strength and operate from its own desires as if it has no need of the Creator. It is the condition and tendency to live life on our own terms—in, of and by ourselves.

The Spirit of God fights against the flesh for our sake. Those who live according to the flesh, Paul tells us, die spiritually. "To set the mind on the flesh is death, but to set the mind on the Spirit is life and peace" (Romans 8:6). We have a spiritual battle against the flesh, which takes spiritual weapons to win.

In addition to cosmic powers and the flesh, the *world*, as a place of sin, is mentioned in the New Testament as being against us. We are tempted by the world—by the evil environment we live in. The world is not only God's good creation but a place of sin and evil. We have a toxic environment. It harms us. It also tempts and seduces us.

It is concerning the world, understood in this way, that John writes: "Do not love the world or the things in the world. The love of the Father is not in those who love the world; for all that is in the world—the desire of the flesh, the desire of the eyes, the pride in riches—comes not from the Father but from the world. And the world and its desire are passing away, but those who do the will of God live forever" (1 John 2:15-17).

Whether it is the power of evil, the flesh or the world, the battle we are engaged in is spiritual, requiring a particular kind of weaponry. We must fight. We will only grow in Christ, if we do battle. But we must fight with the right weapons. We must put on the "armor of God." In Ephesians, this armor includes, truth, righteousness, readiness to proclaim the gospel of peace, faith, salvation and "the sword of the Spirit, which is the word of God" (Ephesians 6:17). We are told to "pray in the Spirit at all times," and to be alert and persevere (Ephesians 6:18). In 1 Thessalonians, Paul says we are to "put on the breastplate of faith and love, and for a helmet the hope of salvation" (1 Thessalonians 5:8).

The battle, in which we are engaged, cannot be waged from fear and anxiety, but from faith; not with hatred and enmity, but love; not with foreboding, but with hope. We must pray our way and depend on the victory that is ours in Christ Jesus. We must care about the truth, being honest especially about ourselves by acknowledging our own unrighteous ways—our own selfishness, lust, greed, pride, fear, and our responsibility for these attitudes. We are not to fight evil with evil but with righteousness and justice. We must learn to operate in the Spirit.

God, who has come to us in Christ Jesus and made himself present in our lives, has given us his Spirit. With his Spirit, comes power for new living. We receive power to overcome the evil one. We receive guidance to see through the temptations of the flesh. The Holy Spirit is called our

Helper, the one who comes along side us and is in and among us. We are not left to fight this battle on our own. God's good news becomes real to us through the work of the Spirit.

The good news is that the battle has already been won through Christ who died for us and was raised for us. In Ephesians, we read that, when Jesus was raised from the dead, he was raised to the right hand of the Father, seated "in the heavenly places" (Ephesians 1:20). The good news is that "in Christ" we have also been seated with him "far above all rule and authority and power and dominion, and above every name that is named, not only in this age but also in the age to come" (Ephesians 1:20-21, 2:6). In Christ, we have authority over powers that used to dictate our lives—including the power of the flesh.

What God has done for us in Christ—the reality of having power, authority and victory—is made available to us by the Holy Spirit. The Spirit makes the work of Christ real to us. Christ's defeat of sin and evil becomes ours. His power over that which would destroy and defeat us becomes ours. Christ's victory and power become real and operative in our lives through the Spirit. Therefore Paul tells us to walk by the Spirit. "If we live by the Spirit, let us also be guided by the Spirit." (Galatians 5:25)

The Spirit is in our lives to lead us. Therefore, be led by the Spirit! Be open to the promptings of the Spirit. There will be times when it is quite clear what is of the flesh and what is of the Spirit. The Spirit will give us the power to walk in the way of life. Simply step out in obedience. When things are not so clear, pray. Pray before taking the next step. Pray with surrender to God's will. Often what clouds our vision is that we are not so sure we want to do God's will. We are being drawn aside by the flesh. We are being tempted. The battle is on. Put on the armor, pray and place your hope and trust in God. Listen for the still small voice of the Spirit. Receive the power of the Spirit that is available and be guided by the Spirit.

We are often tempted when we are going through a trial. (The Greek word used in the New Testament for temptation can also be translated trial.) We are tempted to take the easy way out—the "broad, easy road" that Jesus talks about. Rather than face the trial, go through the struggle and deal with "life on life's terms," we look for an escape hatch. Rather than depend upon God, we depend on a quick fix. The many addictions and false dependencies that entangle us bear witness to the tempting power of the escape hatch. We may have tried to drink, smoke or shoot up our way through trials. We may have spent hours in front of a television set in order to avoid the problems we must finally face. We may have shopped 'til we dropped, dropped out, gamed the system, played other people, lied to ourselves and others, played the blame game and run from our responsibilities.

Now we have come into the new life in Christ Jesus. He tells us to take up our cross and follow him. The trials we used to run from, we are now to face, deal with, or walk through. We are to receive wisdom from on high and trust God. We are to take the hard, narrow road that leads to life. We take up our suffering and keep following the One who has saved us. Our lives are in his hands, in the valley as well as on the mountain top. In the ups and downs, we must learn to trust him. The flesh suggests the easy way out, but we pray, "Where you lead me I will follow."

In the past, we ran from others—ran away from relationships—in order to avoid pain. Even then, we did not really avoid it; we added more. Now we learn that relationships are built through trials, not by avoiding them. Growth means growing pains. The trials and tribulations are no longer simply a threat. We discover that God can use them like a refiner's fire to burn away that which clings to us but does not truly come from him. We are being reshaped and growing toward maturity. We are learning to exercise discipline in relation to our desires, as we take our direction from the Lord.

We are tempted through trials, but trials also give us the opportunity to grow in faith. As we press on in the Lord, trusting in the guidance of the Spirit in the midst of struggles, we are gaining ground against the flesh and the power of evil. We are becoming strong in the Lord. We are developing godly character. Love is gaining room to work in and through us. People that we used to say we could not deal with, we are now praying for and looking for ways to serve. We are experiencing victory in this battle.

And the flesh is having to sit down. We are learning to not pay attention to it but to die to it. By the Spirit, we are obtaining the new life in Christ. We desire to go on. We are becoming anchored. We now know where the victory is. It is in Christ through the power of the Spirit. We are maturing because of the battle—the new battle with a new set of weapons. Thanks be to God.

Guard the good treasure en-
trusted to you, with the help of
the Holy Spirit living in us.

2 Timothy 1:14

4

New Spirit

There is no doing battle against spiritual enemies and no growth in Christ without the Spirit of God. It is important, therefore, to gain understanding of the work of the Spirit in our lives. The new life needs a new spirit.

In the Bible, the word *spirit* is used of humans and God. Paul writes of God's Spirit bearing witness with our spirit that we are children of God (Romans 8:16). Our spirit is made to be touched by God's Spirit. Our spirit aspires; it soars. It reaches out for God. When it turns away from God and settles on some part of God's creation, it has an idol, a false god. Idols only diminish and destroy us, for we were meant to have a relationship with the living God.

The good news of Scripture is that God has come to us in Jesus Christ. God's revelation of himself became flesh and lived among us—"the Word became flesh" (John 1:14). God came to us where we could receive him. He joined himself to our humanity in Christ, so that John could write:

> We declare to you what was from the beginning,
> what we have heard, what we have seen with
> our eyes, what we have looked at and touched
> with our hands, concerning the word of life—
> this life was revealed, and we have seen it and
> testify to it, and declare to you the eternal life
> that was with the Father and was revealed to
> us—we declare to you what we have seen and
> heard so that you also may have fellowship with
> us; and truly our fellowship is with the Father
> and with his Son Jesus Christ. (1 John 1:1-3)

The Creator God did not remain distant and silent but expressed himself among us, united with us, so that the very *word of life* could be heard, seen and touched. God has come to us in our history, and has become joined to our suffering and hurt, and our joys and sorrows. The Reign of God has indeed come near.

Christians have used the term, triune God, to speak of the one God coming to us in three ways: as Creator, as Offspring (God revealed among us) and as Spirit. When we receive God the Creator as he has come to us in his Son, Jesus, it is the Spirit of God who helps us to welcome him. God the Father (and author of all things) comes to us in the Son (God revealed) and opens us to his revelation of himself by the work of God's Spirit. God's Spirit helps us, in other words, to receive Jesus, to follow him and to open ourselves to all that God desires to do in our lives.

The Spirit of God or Holy Spirit is the Helper we need for this new life. Jesus told his followers that he would send the Helper (John 16:7). Some translations of the New Testament translate the Greek word for helper as counselor or advocate or comforter. The Greek word *paraclete* literally means "one who comes along side." In other words, our helper.

The Spirit helps us to welcome and say "yes" to Jesus, the Word of God present as a human being, as well as "yes" to the word of God proclaimed. The Spirit helps us to see, to have spiritual perception. Paul writes of the "eyes of our hearts being enlightened" (Ephesians 1:17). By the Spirit, more is revealed. The Spirit helps us to hear and receive what God is saying to us. Jesus often said, "Let those who have ears to hear, hear." The Spirit gives us ears to hear, so that we discern what God is saying to us and respond in faith and obedience.

For example, we may read a portion of Scripture or hear a sermon, and there may be many things we do not understand or for which we do not see the application, and then, all of a sudden, something is read or heard that we know is for us. God is speaking to us. The word that we are hearing or a verse we are reading is directed to us. It is about us, who we are and what we are going through and our next step. When that happens, it is the Spirit of God bearing witness with our spirit. The word is alive to us and experienced as being "for us."

The Spirit works with the Word, the Word made flesh (Jesus the Christ) and the word proclaimed. The word proclaimed comes from God's witnesses. The "members of the household of God" are "built upon the foundation of the apostles and prophets" (Ephesians 1:19-20). The people of God are built up by the prophetic movement of the Old Testament and the apostolic movement of the New Testament. God reveals himself and his intentions through Moses, Elijah, Elisha, Isaiah, Jeremiah, Ezekiel and the other prophets in the history of Israel in the first part of the Bible and in the second part, through Jesus, God's Anointed, and through the apostles who give witness to Jesus' death and resurrection. God comes to us through word and witness and revelation.

The Spirit continues to work through the Word of God in many ways: through Scripture, through prophetic utterances and revelations among the people of God, through nature, and through who we are becoming as God's children. As we grow in Christ, we become a word in the flesh, that is, God's Word in human experience. We are united to God and give expression to him as we live in him. In prayer, we hear his voice; and in our daily activities and serving, we hear his voice. God speaks to us in a great variety of ways. God's Word is made alive to us by his Spirit.

A Summary of the Spirit's Work

In the sixteenth chapter of John, we are given a concise summary of the work of the Spirit:

> Nevertheless I tell you the truth: it is to your advantage that I go away, for if I do not go away, the Advocate will not come to you; but if I go, I will send him to you. And when he comes, he will prove the world wrong about sin and righteousness and judgment: about sin, because they do not believe in me; about righteousness, because I am going to the Father and you will see me no longer; about judgment, because the ruler of this world has been condemned. I still have many things to say to you, but you cannot bear them now. When the Spirit of truth comes, he will guide you into all the truth; for he will not speak on his own, but will speak whatever he hears, and he will declare to you the things that are to come. He will glorify me, because he will take what is mine and declare it to you. All that the Father has is mine. For this reason I

said that he will take what is mine and declare
it to you. (John 16:7-15)

Jesus sends to us the Advocate (or "Helper") who is the
Spirit of truth. The Spirit proves the world wrong about
sin, righteousness and judgment. The world is wrong about
sin, because it does not believe in Jesus. It does not see the
need for a savior. It thinks that things are not that bad. It
can still save itself. The Spirit comes to show us that things
are much worse than we think. The Spirit convinces and
convicts us of sin. The Spirit reveals the depth of our broken
relationship with God. The Spirit gets past our denials to
reveal to us that our lives have become unmanageable and
that we cannot save ourselves. We need the Savior. When
we experience "conviction of sins" we can be grateful, for
it is God's Spirit at work in us. It is not a work of condemnation but of revelation. When we get caught up in
self-condemnation and self-pity, that is not the Spirit. The
Spirit shows us ourselves in the ugliness of our condition,
not with condemnation but with mercy. The Spirit brings to
us the reality of Jesus who stood before a woman accused
of adultery and surrounded by a group of religious leaders
condemning her to death. Jesus sent away those condemning her and said to her, "I do not condemn you. Go and sin
no more" (John 8:11). So it is that the Spirit convinces us of
our sin in order to, with mercy, send us out to sin no more.
There is, for us, forgiveness and new life.

The Spirit also proves the world wrong about righteousness, because "Jesus goes to the Father and we see him no
longer." While Jesus walked this earth he was a "sign that
contradicts" the ways of this world (Luke 2:34). The world
does not know righteousness. Jesus manifests righteousness
and so does the Spirit of Jesus. The Spirit of truth opens
the eyes of our hearts to what is right, making alive our
consciences to what is of God. The Spirit brings to us what

is on the heart of our Father in heaven, and prompts us according to God's will.

The Spirit proves the world wrong about judgment, "because the ruler of this world has been condemned." The world is cynical about the overcoming of evil. It believes evil must be manipulated and managed because it cannot be conquered. The Spirit of truth, however, convinces us of the defeat of the devil, the ruler of this world. In Christ Jesus, we are more than conquerors (Romans 8:37). We can now overcome evil by the power of the Holy Spirit. We can exercise authority over the evil that used to enslave us. We are engaged in a struggle with sin and evil—sin and evil do not go away, but we are not defenseless in this struggle, for we have the Spirit and Word of God.

The Spirit "guides us into all the truth." The Spirit takes what belongs to Jesus and comes from the Father and declares it to us (John 16:14-15). The Spirit makes Jesus' dying and rising real in our lives. By the power of the Spirit, we grow in dying to the old life and rising to the new. The Spirit makes us alive to God, as Jesus was alive to his Father. The Spirit reminds us of what Jesus has told us and tells us things that we were not at one time able to bear. The Spirit helps us with the next truth that we are able to receive. The Spirit keeps helping us to "get real." God's Spirit puts truth in our inner selves, revealing what has been hidden and leading us into being who God truly intends us to be.

Finally, from this passage, we notice that the Spirit "will declare to us the things that are to come." From the work of God's Spirit in our lives, we receive our hope and purpose and vision. We are given glimpses of what God is about to do—sometimes among God's people, sometimes for ourselves. We receive a vision without which we would perish. We are able to set goals. We have a purpose, a way that moves toward what God has shown us he has in store for us. God gives us a vision for what he is doing and going to do, and God gives us the next steps.

The Spirit in the Body of Christ

Paul writes of the gathered followers of Jesus as the "body of Christ." As the human body has many members with different functions, so the people of God are made up of a diversity of individuals with varying gifts and abilities. The Spirit is active in providing the equipment individuals need for building up the body of Christ and serving the world.

From Paul we learn of gifts of the Spirit that were active in the churches that he served. Among the gifts named are prophecy, teaching, evangelism, knowledge, leadership, administration, service, mercy, healing, miracles, discernment, tongues and interpretation of tongues. He lists others. We can add our own. The main point is that the Spirit activates and stirs up gifts, and we can, as Paul encourages, "strive for the spiritual gifts" (1 Corinthians 14:1). We must reach out for gifts of the Spirit and discover our gifts, so that we may use them to God's glory and to serve others.

The gifts of the Spirit equip us for ministry. They enable us to do what we cannot do in our own strength or with our own natural resources. By means of this spiritual equipment, people are touched, not simply by our "great" opinions or natural abilities, but by the guidance and power of God. People receive healing from God. People hear a word from God directed specifically to them. People are encouraged with the encouragement of God. People are changed by the experience of God's mercy and love. They are cared for just as we have been cared for.

What are we to do to receive these gifts? Open ourselves to the Spirit and to the gifts. Reach out for them. Pray for them. Have others pray for us. Let the Spirit lead and empower us. At various times, in the book of Acts, there are references to Jesus' followers being filled with the Spirit and operating in a gift with power. For example, following a prayer meeting, we read that the disciples were "filled with the Holy Spirit and spoke the word of God with boldness" (Acts 4:31). The experience of being filled with the Spirit involves our yielding to God and submitting ourselves to God's will—"letting go, and letting God."

Being filled with the Spirit not only enables the gifts to flourish, but enables us to overcome the pressures of "the flesh." We are told in Ephesians to "not get drunk with wine, for that is debauchery; but be filled with the Spirit as you sing psalms and hymns and spiritual songs among yourselves, singing and making melody to the Lord in your hearts, giving thanks to God the Father at all times and for everything in the name of our Lord Jesus Christ" (Ephesians 5:18-20). Being filled with the Spirit gives us power to overcome the appetites, disoriented tendencies, desires and attitudes which Paul calls the *flesh*. In the above passage, this being filled with the Spirit involves us in the act of worship. Through Spirit-filled worship, we discover great power for living the new life.

The Holy Spirit does great work in our lives within the body of Christ, the gathered community of God's people. Yes, the Spirit comes to be in us, but the Spirit also comes to be among us in the gathered community, where various gifts are being exercised in ministry to others. In the worshiping community, we are built up in faith, hope and love. We share our needs and confess our sins and pray for one another. We receive healing and deliverance, guidance and power.

We grow. The Holy Spirit produces fruit in our lives. "The fruit of the Spirit is love, joy, peace, patience, kindness, generosity, faithfulness, gentleness, and self-control" (Galatians

5:22-23). As we are filled with the Spirit and led by the Spirit, we walk into the new life, gaining a new character as God's children, receiving new ways of thinking and acting. God is giving us everything we need to mature in him.

5

New Thinking

When we come to live in Christ, we gain a new way of thinking. As our lives come to be centered in him, our thoughts increasingly become formed by the "heavenly call" that we have in him. We are new creations, with a new view and new ways. We are to be of the same mind with others who have come to know him. If we "think differently about anything," or if we are not seeing some things as God would have us see them, God will reveal that to us. The Spirit will help us to new ways of thinking.

New Perspectives

Where we take our stand forms our horizons. The point from which we view things determines what we tend to see. If the point at which we have taken our stand is our own pleasure, then we see the world in terms of our pleasure. We tend to do what feels good and avoid pain. If our commitment is to personal power, then we view the world in terms of opportunities to gain power. Whatever we are fundamentally committed to is either going to be an idol or God. If our basic commitment in life is to ourselves or an image of ourselves as the center of things, then we have an idol, and our perspective is formed by that idol. If, on the other hand, our lives have been turned over to the living God, our perspective is becoming formed by our trust in God.

If we have turned (and are turning) from idols to God, our perspectives are changing. If we have begun to know the reality that is ours in Christ Jesus who is the door into faith in God, our thinking is going through a transformation. We are starting to see ourselves differently—as sinners, yes, but as forgiven and loved. We are no longer only victims, but victors. There is power in our lives for overcoming those things that have dominated and diminished our lives. And life has meaning. We are gaining purpose and direction, and it is not coming from our self-absorption and willfulness, but from the Creator's will for us.

We can cooperate with this change that the Spirit of God is working in us. Our gaining a new perspective and new thoughts, however, does not mean the old thoughts simply disappear. There is a battle going on as our thinking changes. Paul writes about this—although for him this battle is not only waged by us as individuals but within the body of Christ: "Indeed, we live as human beings, but we do not wage war according to human standards; for the weapons of our warfare are not merely human, but they have divine power to destroy strongholds. We destroy arguments and every proud obstacle raised up against the knowledge of God, and we take every thought captive to obey Christ" (2 Corinthians 10:3-5).

We are engaged in a battle against false thinking that instigates false living. There are various kinds of false thinking in our lives that are strongholds, ingrained and habitual. They have us in bondage. Some are philosophical in nature. They come from a previous world-view that did not include God. We had lived as if everything was up to us. We had held the reins of our existence. When trouble came, we had felt it was up to us to straighten everything out. This perspective had been a source of anxiety and remains so as this way of thinking lingers. We have to be reminded daily that our lives are in God's hands. We are to trust him in the midst of things that we do not understand and cannot control.

Some thoughts from the old life are very personal: We have thought about ourselves too highly or too lowly. We have viewed ourselves above others or suffered from low self-esteem. We judged others with little mercy or lived under our own self-condemnation. We have carried around thoughts about ourselves arising from relationships and experiences that demeaned us. These thoughts gave us no hint of how God thinks about us, but they colored all our thinking and doing.

We now must learn to cooperate with the work of the Spirit of God as we discover God's grace and mercy, his steadfast love that claims us as his children, and that has us looking at others in our lives differently, with compassion. When the old thoughts show up, we have to take them captive and make them obey Christ as we open our hearts to receive what God is saying to us. We have to say no to the old thoughts and yes to what God is saying. We must let God speak personally to us—his thoughts about us becoming our thoughts about ourselves, and his word to us directing our thinking and actions. It is a matter of trusting in him now, rather than trusting thoughts that have been ours for many years.

New Behavior

With changing thoughts come changing behavior. We are seeing ourselves and others differently, and so we are acting differently. We find we are becoming more forgiving towards others, less judging and less controlling. God is judge; we are not. God is Lord; we are not. In him all things hold together, therefore we do not need to keep trying to hold our lives together. We can trust and act from that trust.

We are recognizing abusive behavior and turning from it. We are more circumspect about our desires. We are realizing that they cannot simply dictate our lives. The children of God are led by the Spirit. We care about the truth and about doing what is right. The ten commandments are making more sense to us.

If we are coming out of an addiction, we are becoming sensitive to other kinds of addictions. We are recognizing obsessions and areas of our lives that were out of control because we had no anchor. We have an anchor now, and we are gaining freedom from former obsessions.

We are being raised up into love. We are being raised up into God in whose image we were made, and God is love—unconditional love. God loves us no matter where we have been or what we have done. God loves us because God is love. That love is entering our lives as we are open to God.

How we encounter others is changed by our experience of God's kind of love. People in our lives are not simply objects of interest in so far as they affect us, but are to be loved for who they are as creatures of God. It is no longer simply a matter of "you scratch my back, I scratch yours." God's love goes out to those who cannot give us anything in return, and we are being raised up into that kind of love. Constrained by this love, we cannot make others into mere objects of our desires.

Sexual desire, as with all desires, must now become grounded in and supported by the love of God. All expressions of our bodies, including sexual expression, is to be the communication of the love of God. Love is the foundation of everything, as God is the foundation of all. Entering into a sexual relationship with another person is never merely an action of our bodies. We cannot separate the physical from the spiritual; our bodies (through which we express ourselves) are from God in whose image we were made. What we do bodily is the means by which we give expression to the love and faithfulness of God. We have come to know intimacy with God through God's love and commitment to us.

In our relationships with one another, we cannot separate true intimacy from commitment, anymore than we can have relationships without faithfulness. God is committed and faithful to us. It is for good reason that, when Christians have talked about sexual relations, they have talked about marriage, covenant or commitment to lifelong faithfulness. Sexual intimacy becomes an expression of whole-life, whole-self commitment. In fact, in Ephesians, marriage is seen as a symbol of the union of Christ and the church, with all the faithfulness, caring, and serving which that represents. When there is faithfulness and commitment in relationships, the human community gains health and children are nurtured. The commandment, "Thou shalt not commit adultery" takes on new depth of meaning for us, as we are being grounded in love.

Not only is our neighbor's wife or husband not to become the object of our desire, but neither is our neighbor's property or business or position. Love does not steal or obtain by fraud or covet what belongs to another. On the contrary, love helps our neighbor with that which belongs to him or her, including encouragement and support with his or her calling and career. Love has us working for justice when institutions and corporations are defrauding people of their homes and livelihoods. Love has us active in pursuing justice in governments, businesses and institutions.

Love "does not bear false witness against our neighbor." The Bible has much to say concerning how we talk about the people in our lives. We are not to gossip about one another. If we have something against someone, we are not to go and talk about that person with someone else, but go to that person and work things out. We "are to do unto others as we would want them to do unto us." We are not to harm them with words or actions. We are, instead, to help them, serve them and show compassion for them. Jesus even tells us that we are to love our enemies and pray for them. God's love has no limits. God loves all, and his love is being poured into our hearts.

> Love is patient; love is kind; love is not envi-
> ous or boastful or arrogant or rude. It does not
> insist on its own way; it is not irritable or re-
> sentful; it does not rejoice in wrongdoing, but
> rejoices in the truth. It bears all things, believes
> all things, hopes all things, endures all things.
> (1 Corinthians 13:4-7)

Love keeps attending to relationships and caring for others. The love of God does not diminish. There is always more. It is ours as we continue to be open to the work of God's Spirit in us. We are being changed into lovers of others. God is doing this. Grow in him and we grow in love. If we keep growing up as God's children, we will love more, and it will be manifest in our behavior. We will be bearing with the struggles, hurts and sins of others in ways that we had never imagined for ourselves. We will believe in God for others and for their change and transformation and healing. We will speak words of hope to them and encourage them. We will go through trials to serve others in love, because God is love and we reside in him.

Speaking the truth in love, we
must grow up in every way into
him who is the head, into Christ.

Ephesians 4:15

6

New Growth

I know from various experiences with a small vegetable garden, that I can prepare the ground and plant small seedlings, do little else and still get vegetables. As long as there is periodic rain, even with the weeds and insect predators, I will have something to eat. But I also know that if I weed the garden, take precautions against predators, add fertilizer and water, I will have more and larger vegetables. That which has been planted has a propensity for living and growing no matter how much I neglect it. But it does much better when I nourish it.

This is also true for our new life in Christ. Just as weeds, insect predators and lack of nutrients stunt growth in my vegetable garden, so spiritual weeds, predators and lack of nourishment constrict the life that flows from Christ. We come to Christ with weeds that are choking the life out of us—living as if life consisted in the abundance of possessions, or entangled in a dysfunctional or abusive relationship—as abused or abuser, or burdened by guilt and filled with hurt and anger or stressed out by trying to hold our lives together, or strangled in our own self-satisfaction and self-righteousness. There are aspects of our habitual ways of operating that are like weeds and predators—the ways we deceive ourselves and others in order to avoid the truth and deny what is happening to ourselves. Sometimes couples come to me whose relationships have become destructive, hurtful and utterly broken, and they express surprise at how badly things have deteriorated after having started out so very much in love. But the seeds, the destructive modes of operation, were always there. They simply ignored them or denied their existence.

We come to the new life with weeds and predators and "suckers" from the old life. I had a neighbor who grew beautiful tomato plants producing large healthy tomatoes. He showed me what he did. He cut off the "suckers," the branches that sucked energy from the plant while providing little or no fruit. Something like that must happen for us spiritually. Those branches in our lives that simply sap away spiritual life must be pruned. Jesus says,

> I am the true vine, and my Father is the vine-grower. He removes every branch in me that bears no fruit. Every branch that bears fruit he prunes to make it bear more fruit. You have already been cleansed by the word that I have spoken to you. Abide in me as I abide in you. Just as the branch cannot bear fruit by itself unless it abides in the vine, neither can you unless you abide in me. I am the vine, you are the branches. Those who abide in me and I in them bear much fruit, because apart from me you can do nothing (John 15:1-5).

We flourish and bear fruit when we abide in Christ and are cleansed by his word. (The Greek word for cleansed can also be translated pruned.) God speaks to us, addresses us personally, and his word cuts. It prunes that which is false and that which takes away from the true self that we are becoming in Christ. There are behaviors and ways of thinking about ourselves that have no place in our lives in Christ. When God cuts, we must be let go. Past sins must be repented from and past hurts must be healed.

Growth in Christ does not, however, happen simply by removal. We must daily receive the new life. We must receive the nutrients of the word, sacraments and fellowship. There are these two aspects of growing up in Christ: (1) Get rid of the weeds and suckers. (2) Receive nourishment.

Get Rid of the Weeds and Suckers

We cannot grow in our new life in Christ without giving some attention to the weeds and suckers. Over the years, I have ministered to women who have been abused, women who have prostituted themselves to maintain their drug habit, men who have used prostitutes, men and women coming out of addictions, men with a history of drug dealing and gang involvement, men and women who have spent time in prison, children and adults in dysfunctional family situations, professionals with middle-class values overly concerned with property and status, elitists, pleasure seekers, as well as long-time self-righteous church goers and individuals who have made a habit of judging others from their particular moralistic pedestal and generally people caught up in racism, classism, materialism and hedonism—among other "isms." What is clear is that we all have the same fundamental struggles and needs.

All of us have weeds and suckers that would rob us of the spiritual energy for growth in the new life. We have had to name the weeds and suckers for what they were and let God root out and prune them. I have seen God graciously do just that. I have witnessed women who were beaten down, be raised up and have their self-esteem restored. It has happened in the community God forms, where there is support, love, words of encouragement and God's truth about ourselves. I have seen long-time addicts delivered from their addictions and maintained in their recovery by a supportive community and the truth that helps us to "live life on life's terms." I have witnessed the self-righteous humbled by the conviction of their sin so that they have realized we are all in the same boat and in need of the same mercy of God. I have seen class distinctions and racism break down as the dividing walls of society fall under the impact of God's reign breaking into our lives.

The starting point for getting rid of weeds and suckers is acknowledging them. When we were living far from the God who saves, we were trying to save ourselves by "saving face," by ignoring the true nature of our problems, by hiding from others and ourselves our faults and hurts. We tried to deal with pain by covering it up or drowning it out or talking around it or repressing it. But the pain and dissonance did not go away because we ignored them. The suckers still sucked the life out of us.

When we came to know God through Jesus Christ, we found that we were welcomed and accepted despite all the brokenness of our lives. God's love assured us that it would not let us go. It was steadfast and unconditional. The things that we could not formerly face and address, we can today. One of the things that I have noticed in counseling individuals is that they will tell me things they have told no one else as long as they know that they are accepted and loved and not judged. We are released from shame by

God's loving mercy. God does not count our sin against us, nor does he put us down for hurting. God forgives and heals.

When we acknowledge the weeds and suckers, when we let God's Spirit bring them to light, we take a great step. We begin to take part in God's work of removal and healing. For some past experiences that still hang around sucking life from us, we receive relief as we forgive others who have sinned against us. That is at least part of our healing, and may involve a process that includes anger, sharing with others, praying, letting go, and acceptance. Continuing to hear the truth God speaks into our lives, that we are loved and have great worth before God, brings further healing. Living the new life and responding to God's purpose for us, provides daily healing.

When we have been hurt by others, we often hurt others and have actions we need to repent from or ask forgiveness for. That also forms part of the removal of suckers that have been drawing off the life that God has for us. Sometimes we need to find another Christian, especially a mature Christian, and confess before another human being our sin and brokenness, getting specific where appropriate. Choose a Christian who knows about speaking God's word of forgiveness. We do not need someone who is going to say, "It's not that bad." We have said that before to ourselves, and it has not helped. We need someone who will acknowledge our guilt, shame and sin for what it is, and speak God's forgiveness and mercy.

The healing that God brings does not take away the hurt or brokenness as if it had never been. I notice that when I cut a sucker off one of my tomato plants, a wound remains. (The risen Jesus pointed out the scars in his hands and side.) Whatever remains from past hurts and sins, becomes part of God's purpose in our lives today. God will use the healed wounds in our serving and ministering to others.

> Blessed be the God and Father of our Lord Jesus
> Christ, the Father of mercies and the God of all
> consolation, who consoles us in all our affliction,
> so that we may be able to console those who
> are in any affliction with the consolation with
> which we ourselves are consoled by God. (2
> Corinthians 1:3-4)

With God's ministry of healing and comfort and encouragement that we have received, we minister to others.

Receive Nourishment

Much of the healing and restoration we experience in our
lives simply comes from the nourishment we receive. The
water, fertilizer and sunlight the plant receives gives it the
health and strength to overcome weeds and predators.

We must also receive nourishment to grow in the new
life. Christian baptism is a symbol of our new beginning. It
expresses our drowning to the old life that we may arise
into the new. We are buried with Christ, so that we may
also rise with him.

> Do you not know that all of us who have been
> baptized into Christ Jesus were baptized into his
> death? 4 Therefore we have been buried with
> him by baptism into death, so that, just as Christ
> was raised from the dead by the glory of the
> Father, so we too might walk in newness of life.
> (Romans 6:3-4)

In baptism, we are initiated into the reality of dying and
rising. Buried with Christ, we are like a seed planted in
fertile soil so that new life might spring forth and grow and
bear fruit. "Very truly, I tell you, unless a grain of wheat

falls into the earth and dies, it remains just a single grain; but if it dies, it bears much fruit" (John 12:24).

The seed of new life must be nurtured. It must receive the water of Word and Spirit. We must be very intentional about this. If I want a garden that bears much fruit, I will have to water it regularly—especially in times of drought—whether I feel like it or not. What is true for my vegetable garden is also true for the garden of my soul. It needs tending.

Christians, therefore, talk about "spiritual disciplines." By the word "disciplines," we mean activities for nourishing the new life which are not dependent upon our feelings, attitudes and inner state, but upon daily habits. We carve time out of our daily and weekly schedules for prayer, Bible and devotional reading, solitude and gatherings with other sisters and brothers in Christ for sharing.

If I care about my physical health, I will attend to the needs of my body. At the least, I will give it food and water from time to time, without which I cannot remain alive. Of course, I can also give care to *what* I eat. Some foods are more nutritious than others. Some, like refined sugar, offer virtually no nutrition, and some (animal fat) will clog my arteries. If I have had a habit of eating food high in sugar and fat and my body has developed a craving for sugar and fat, I tend to respond to those cravings. If I am going to nurture my body back to health (and healthy eating), I will have to change my habits and thus my cravings.

Something like that has to happen for us spiritually. Our God-given spiritual cravings have come to be misplaced. Instead of openness toward and trust in God, we have been open to and put our trust in idols. We have had the habit of seeking life in all the wrong places—pleasure, power, status, wealth, comfort, etc. Words like lust, greed, arrogance and coveting give expression to the misplaced orientation of our spirit.

Now that we have come into the new life through Christ, we are experiencing desire for God and life in the Spirit. And yet the old desires and cravings do not simply disappear. When I found out many years ago that my cholesterol was high and I had to change my diet, my craving for pastrami sandwiches did not disappear and the joy of eating salads immediately take hold. It was only as I disciplined myself to eat differently that my body's cravings began to change.

The new life in the Spirit needs new habits. It needs to be daily nurtured. Old habits must be exchanged with new habits. Instead of watching a particular TV program that simply appeals to "my flesh," I may need to read a devotional book. Instead of staying up late to watch the late, late movie on Saturday night, I need to make sure I get my rest in preparation for worship with the gathered community of faith on Sunday. I must put Bible reading and prayer into my life daily and displace other activities in the process. I need to take time to be alone and still before God. As I am carving out room for the Spirit, I find that I can replace with silence the "need" to always have a TV or radio on.

I learn to have "holy conversations." Instead of entering into gossip, I pray and wait on the Lord for words that are in keeping with the new life. I may find myself speaking less and listening more—and saying more that is significant when I do speak. I seek life in conversations with true sharing with others, rather than titillation. God is about building up relationships and community.

By spiritual discipline, we get intentional about growing up into the new life and bearing fruit. Here are disciplines that will change our life and life-style:

- Daily Bible reading
- Alone time for prayer
- Weekly small group Bible study

- Prayer meetings
- Prayer partners
- Worship gatherings
- Retreats
- Fasting
- Living simply
- Serving
- Working for justice
- Controlling the tongue

A few of these may need some explanation. *Fasting* accompanies prayer as a way of setting aside other activities or disciplining our appetites so that we may focus on what God wants to say to us. We may fast from food for a period of time, or TV or shopping or any number of things that take up our time. In this way, we gain discipline in our seeking God.

Making a practice of *living simply* disciplines our inordinate desire for more things or experiences in our lives. By "living simply" I mean being intentional about what we really need or what fits with our experience of God's call in our lives. Living simply means making decisions that produce a life-style that is oriented to and streamlined for God's purposes for us.

Serving and *working for justice* take us out of our preoccupation with ourselves and bring our focus on the needs of others. We discipline ourselves to notice the needs of others and respond. We allow ourselves to be inconvenienced by others, and we gain a healthier perspective of ourselves. Some of the things that we take so very seriously we learn are simply not that serious when we are reaching out to help others. Working to make things right that are wrong on a wider social level engages us beyond our own often petty concerns. God calls us to be light in the darkness, salt that seasons and yeast that leavens (affects) the whole.

In other words, we are to be change agents in our society. Involvement in actions for social justice can be an important spiritual discipline.

Above all, the spiritual disciplines that go to the heart of the change God brings involve prayer, sharing in the word, worship, giving thanks and praising God. Being intentional about daily submitting ourselves to God and his will is a spiritual discipline. Thanking God in all circumstances is a spiritual discipline. Glorifying God (instead of ourselves) is a spiritual discipline. Humbling ourselves in prayer, acknowledging that we cannot live without daily communion with God is a spiritual discipline.

We receive nourishment in the new life through spiritual disciplines, just as we receive nourishment for our bodies as we discipline our habits for eating and exercise, going to the doctor for checkups, getting the rest we need and listening to what our bodies are telling us. We must give space in our lives for listening to what the Spirit is telling us.

"Come to him, a living stone, though rejected by mortals yet chosen and precious in God's sight, and like living stones, let yourselves be built into a spiritual house, to be a holy priesthood, to offer spiritual sacrifices acceptable to God through Jesus Christ."

1 Peter 2:4-5

7

New Community

We are not disconnected individuals like so many islands separated and isolated, existing unto themselves. God created us for community. We cannot exist without relationships, the support of family, the dynamics of love between ourselves and others. We have a fundamental need to let ourselves be built into a spiritual household.

The early Christians came together in house gatherings. The term, "household of God," arose from the experience of Christians meeting in households. At times, all the members of a household became believers and were baptized, and they opened their house to other believers. Together they became the family of God. They ministered to one another as mediators of God's word and love. They grew up into Christ together. They experienced the dividing walls that existed in society breaking down within their gatherings.

When Paul wrote to the gatherings of God in Corinth, he wrote to address various issues, especially the problem of divisions. There were cliques formed around personalities, spiritual gifts, differing opinions and class. This last issue was not a surprising one given the class distinctions of Roman society. The Christians in Corinth represented a cross section of society. "Consider your own call, brothers and sisters: not many of you were wise by human standards, not many were powerful, not many were of noble birth" (1 Corinthians 1:26). Most were not educated, many must have been slaves or freedmen, but some were also powerful and of noble birth (but "not many").

Under the power of the Spirit, they were experiencing the dividing walls of society coming down. A slave could receive a gift of prophecy or a gift of miracles or a calling to leadership. It has been noted that, among the apparent leaders from Corinth mentioned by Paul, there were "Fortunatus and Achaicus." The use of nicknames, such as these, indicates possible slaves or freedmen. The experience of the Spirit in the early church was leveling the harsh divisions of Roman society, so that Paul could write "There is no longer Jew or Greek, there is no longer slave or free, there is no longer male and female; for all of you are one in Christ Jesus" (Galatians 3:28).

I am reminded of the Azusa Street Revival and the birth of the Pentecostal movement beginning in 1906 through the leadership of an African American pastor, William J. Seymour. The outpouring of the Spirit brought about not only an abundance of spiritual gifts but, in the words of the time, the breaking of the "color line." People of all races, rich and poor flowed to Azusa Street. Women were encouraged in leadership and "status" was based on the work of the Spirit. The dividing walls of society were coming down. And yet, eventually, racism as a force again raised its ugly head especially through a white preacher and former teacher of Seymour, Charles Parham, who had been invited to the Azusa Street Mission.

Something like that was happening in Corinth. The church had experienced profound unity in the Spirit, only to have the forces of classism effectively cause problems among the brothers and sisters in Christ. Paul exercised apostolic leadership in calling upon the Corinthian Christians to acknowledge the one "body" of Christ. In their "love feasts," when they remembered the last meal Jesus had with his followers and partook of the bread and the cup, the wealthy were not to sit down at the meal before slaves who came after finishing their work. Some had been eating well and even getting drunk at these meals, while others were going hungry. To this Paul warns the church: "For all who eat and drink without discerning the body, eat and drink judgment against themselves" (1 Corinthians 11:29). They are individually members of one body in Christ, and they are to discern that body and operate appropriately, in love.

We are called into a *new* community. "If one member suffers, all suffer together with it; if one member is honored, all rejoice together with it" (1 Corinthians 12:26). The dividing walls of hostility have come down *in Christ*. The unity that has escaped the world is now to be found in Christ. The issue now is to truly live "in Christ." Let the Christ reality take over, and do not succumb to the former life "in the world."

We become members of this new community by coming to Christ and "like living stones, let [ourselves] be built into a spiritual house" (1 Peter 2:5). We grow into the reality of this new community as we remain in Christ. This new community is to demonstrate the love of God, and therefore it must keep opening itself to Christ. It is to be a place of nurture for new Christians, and therefore it must mature in Christ. Each member has a responsibility to grow in Christ, not only for his or her own sake, but for the sake of others.

Sometimes new Christians are, at first, impressed by the love of the brothers and sisters in the new community, only to find—given time—expressions of jealousy, selfishness, controlling ways, and other forms of brokenness. The new community, which shares in Christ's love, also carries within it seeds for its destruction. After all, the members bring into the fellowship the same sins and hurts that all of humanity is familiar with. They are, however, on a journey into new life, and the new community is an integral part of that journey. Christ's community is desperately needed for continuing into the new life.

Therefore, those seeds that, if left to grow, will destroy the community must be addressed. The beautiful thing is that within Christ's community there exists everything necessary for addressing the problems that arise. There is the Spirit of Christ and instruction in the ways of healing and building relationships. Consider the kinds of instructions handed down to us in the New Testament:

> Bear with one another and, if anyone has a complaint against another, forgive each other; just as the Lord has forgiven you, so you also must forgive. (Colossians 3:13)

> So when you are offering your gift at the altar, if you remember that your brother or sister has something against you, leave your gift there before the altar and go; first be reconciled to your brother or sister, and then come and offer your gift. (Matthew 5:23-24)

> If another member of the church sins against you, go and point out the fault when the two of you are alone. If the member listens to you, you have regained that one. But if you are not listened to, take one or two others along with you, so that every word may be confirmed by the

evidence of two or three witnesses. (Matthew 18:15-16)

Welcome one another, therefore, just as Christ has welcomed you, for the glory of God. (Romans 15:7)

Lead a life worthy of the calling to which you have been called, with all humility and gentleness, with patience, bearing with one another in love, making every effort to maintain the unity of the Spirit in the bond of peace. (Ephesians 4:1-2)

The new community is a place where Christians can practice Christ-love. They receive training for loving others out in the world as they live it among each other. They learn to turn away from the practices of judging others. (When churches become places of judgmentalism and self-righteousness, they have indeed moved far from the love of Christ.) Within the community of faith, Christians learn to repent from controlling and deceitful ways, holding grudges, looking for ways to "get back," or get their way. Instead they grow in responding to the needs of others. They become more understanding of human failings while at the same time lifting up the power of God's Spirit for overcoming those failings. They learn to show mercy even as God has been merciful to them. The Spirit of Christ is operating in gatherings of people where these things are present.

It is important to "let ourselves be built into a spiritual house." Some Christians get impatient with the growing pains and move from one church experience to another, never letting themselves be built into a spiritual house. We need to put down roots, to gain staying power, so that we may grow. Above all, we must learn to respond to the call of God in our lives, rather than the flighty desires of our flesh. The Spirit leads us deep into community and in the use of our gifts so that we are ministering to others and being used by God to build community.

If we desire to go more deeply into the reality of the new community, we must be on a journey of discovering our spiritual gifts. "Pursue love and strive for the spiritual gifts" (1 Corinthians 14:1). Be open to the Holy Spirit, be reaching out for gifts of the Spirit, and discover what even now God is putting into your life. Be led by the Spirit into the work of serving others. Let God use you to minister to others. There is a place that fits you in the "spiritual building" where you will be able to use your gifts to the glory of God and with joy. Discover that place. Discover that ministry.

God put this power to work in Christ when he raised him from the dead and seated him at his right hand in the heavenly places, far above all rule and authority and power and dominion, and above every name that is named, not only in this age but also in the age to come.

Ephesians 2:20-21

8

New Authority

In our congregation, we have seen people's lives changed by the power of God. There have been those who have received healing for past hurts, deliverance from addictions, changed life-styles, restoration in relationships, self-worth, hope for the future and renewed vision for living. God "has rescued us from the power of darkness and transferred us into the kingdom of his beloved Son" (Colossians 1:13). This work of God has become ours. We have learned to take authority in the name of Christ over that which has had us bound.

Growth in Christ involves walking in our victory in Christ. Growth happens as we fight the good fight of faith with the new authority that is ours. Growth happens through spiritual conflict in which the old dies and the new comes to life. In this conflict, there are powers arrayed against us. God wants us to know that we have authority over these powers through Jesus Christ.

There are a number of Greek words used for power and authority in the New Testament. Clearly, the issue of power is central to the message. Jesus operates with authority. He takes authority over unclean spirits, diseases and, in the calming of the storm, nature. We see Jesus' authority exercised in the healing of a man who is paralyzed:

> "But so that you may know that the Son of Man has authority on earth to forgive sins"—he then said to the paralytic—"Stand up, take your bed and go to your home." And he stood up and went to his home. When the crowds saw it, they were filled with awe, and they glorified God, who had given such authority to human beings (Matthew 9:6-8).

God gives "such authority to human beings." It is given to us. "Then Jesus summoned his twelve disciples and gave them authority over unclean spirits, to cast them out, and to cure every disease and every sickness" (Matthew 10:1).

Generally in the New Testament, references to "powers" have to do with evil forces that go beyond our own personal evil, unclean spirits, "spiritual forces of evil" (Ephesians 6:12). It is clear, however, that we are to take authority over all forces that would take us away from the new life in Christ—especially "the flesh" and the world. In Christ, we have authority to do that.

The Flesh

We are to exercise authority over what Paul calls "the flesh." Our condition can be described as basically warped. We carry around with us desires and attitudes and values that are idolatrous. We have a tendency to live life turned in on ourselves and relying on our own strength. This is what

Paul means by "the flesh." This condition works against the new life. Therefore, we are not to set our minds on the flesh, but instead set our minds on the Spirit. We are to take authority over the flesh by living according to the Spirit. The Spirit of God can overcome the flesh.

> For those who live according to the flesh set their minds on the things of the flesh, but those who live according to the Spirit set their minds on the things of the Spirit. To set the mind on the flesh is death, but to set the mind on the Spirit is life and peace. (Romans 8:5-6)

When we succumb to the flesh and follow its dictates, we must "take authority" by again repenting and turning to our Lord, receiving his forgiveness, and trusting in him. Repenting and trusting become a way of life in Christ.

We keep taking authority over the flesh as we walk by the Spirit instead of by the dictates of the flesh. We must learn to live attentive to the Spirit and discerning of what the Spirit is telling us over against the flesh. By doing so, we live as victors in Christ.

The World

In addition to the flesh, we must daily take authority over environmental triggers. We are influenced by the world around us. It is powerfully present to tempt and entrap us. It would have us turn from serving the creator to serving our own appetites and desires. We are not to "love the world or the things of the world" (1 John 2:15). We are not to wrap our hearts around the tendencies and thinking and dominant ways of society—ways that ignore the creator and idolize ourselves.

We find our authority over the ways of the world in the cross of Christ: "May I never boast of anything except the cross of our Lord Jesus Christ, by which the world has been crucified to me, and I to the world" (Galatians 6:14). The key is being "in Christ." In Christ, we have died to the seductive and harmful ways of the world, for in Christ the ways of the world are dead. We operate with authority over the world as we remain in Christ and in him die to the "triggers" and temptations of the world.

At times, the experience of dying to the world involves suffering. It can be painful to let go of ways of operating that have been deeply embedded in our identity and to walk away from that which we used to live in. But we know now that there is no life in the ways of the world. As Christ died to the temptations of the world, so now, in Christ, we die. We die daily, so that we might rise daily. As we do so, we are taking authority over the world.

Past Sin

Past sin and its consequences often exercise power over us. Feelings of guilt and condemnation rob us of joy. Unacknowledged guilt is often expressed in self-righteousness and judgmentalism. Guilt feelings blind us to God's grace and loving guidance.

We exercise authority over past sin and guilt through confession and forgiveness. God's forgiveness sets us free from the debilitating bondage of guilt. "In him we have redemption through his blood, the forgiveness of our trespasses, according to the riches of his grace that he lavished on us" (Ephesians 1:7-8).

God has given us steps to take: (1) Acknowledge the guilt. (2) Accept God's forgiveness. (3) Where possible, make amends. Guilt loses its power over us when it is acknowledged and forgiven.

> "Then I acknowledged my sin to you, and I did not hide my iniquity; I said, 'I will confess my transgressions to the Lord', and you forgave the guilt of my sin" (Psalm 32:5).

Where we have wronged another, and there is opportunity to make things right, we need to take it. After all, God is about relationships, and he would have us be reconciled where that is possible.

Past Hurts

The sins of others affect us. Our past can determine our present feelings about ourselves and direct our decisions and actions. Parenting methods, demeaning words, stereotypes, emotional and physical abuse in the past, all have an impact on how we feel about ourselves today and how we function in the world. Traumas from war, torture, rape, sexual abuse, can be especially debilitating. There are some hurts that need the attention of counselors and mental health care-givers.

The past does not just go away. It remains with us. When there are festering wounds, the past sometimes continues to be experienced in the form of physical and emotional ailments. There is great need for healing. There is help for the wounds of past hurts through supportive relationships, the community of faith, seeking help, prayer, acknowledging the hurt and where it comes from, forgiving those who have hurt us.

We can look upon Jesus as our healer. We can let Jesus enter into the past which we still carry with us. In prayer, we can let him speak to that past, let him release us from past hurts, let him help us with forgiving those who have sinned against us. We can use our imagination in prayer: What is Jesus saying to us as we bring our hurt to him? Are we able to forgive? Can we ask Jesus to help us with forgiving?

Forgiveness releases us. It is the primary means by which we take authority over past hurts. Forgiveness is powerful for emotional and mental health, and it is a gift from God. Reach out and receive it.

Disease

> Are any among you suffering? They should pray. Are any cheerful? They should sing songs of praise. Are any among you sick? They should call for the elders of the church and have them pray over them, anointing them with oil in the name of the Lord. The prayer of faith will save the sick, and the Lord will raise them up; and anyone who has committed sins will be forgiven. Therefore confess your sins to one another, and pray for one another, so that you may be healed. (James 5:13-16)

Jesus views physical illness as belonging to the dominion of the evil one. Whether physical illness has spiritual or emotional roots, whether it involves a break down of the immune system and physical disorders, it is seen as something from which people are to be delivered. Jesus heals people because he has compassion on them. We are to continue the ministry of Jesus through his community out of compassion for suffering people.

At the heart of our authority over disease is the prayer of faith. To those Jesus healed, he often said, "Your faith has made you well." The faith of Christ's community connects the power of God with the needs of community members. We must pray for each other's healing. There is great power in the community of faith for the healing of its members. James encourages those who cannot be present with the gathered community to call for leaders to come and pray for them. "The prayer of faith will save the sick, and the Lord will raise them up."

Social Sickness

Powerful sinful social structures bear down upon the lives of people, often unseen. Though hidden, they exert relentless and oppressive influence:

- Unjust, inequitable funding of public education
- Unrepresentative government
- Discriminatory hiring practices
- Discriminatory housing practices
- Discrimination in the availability of health services
- Unjust criminal justice system
- Biased sentencing of convicted persons
- Corporate environmental pollution
- A national security state that quickly goes to war
- Unjust and corrupt ecclesiastical structures

We take authority over social sickness when we do justice in Jesus' name, when we "let justice roll down like waters, and righteousness like an everflowing stream" (Amos 5:24). Injustice must be confronted. God calls forth witnesses against evil and oppressive ways of society and its institutions. Christ's community is called to stand up with others as witnesses. As we come to know God's intentions for humankind, we must bear witness. If we are not ourselves being discriminated against (the social system more or less "works" for us), we must bear witness for the sake of others who are experiencing discrimination.

Doing justice means making right that which is wrong. We must work to understand and "see" the wrong. We must not only see the wrong, but must work to correct it. We must encourage and gather others to the task. We are called to be salt, light and yeast. As yeast affects the whole loaf of bread, we are to influence every aspect of this world.

Spiritual Forces Of Evil

We are up against "spiritual forces of evil in the heavenly places" (Ephesians 6:12). Scripture knows of evil greater than our own as "demonic." Demonic evil has found many forms of expression throughout history and across cultures. Evil has troubled, oppressed and bound individuals, groups and nations.

The good news, however, is that, in Christ, the community of faith has been given power and authority over all evil. There is deliverance in Jesus' name. Are you troubled by the power of evil in your life? Seek the prayers and counsel of God's people, especially that of mature Christians.

Above all, as we grow in the truth, living in the truth, and walking by the Spirit, the forces of deception and evil lose their foothold. As we turn ourselves over to God and refuse to be conformed to this world but are being transformed by the renewal of our minds (Romans 12:1-2), evil is being dislodged. God reigns, and we are secure in him. And we are defeating the evil one through Christ.

Whether we are dealing with the temptations of flesh and world, or past hurt and sin, or disease, or evil, personal, social and demonic, there is power available to take authority and to overcome. Operate in the authority given to you in Christ Jesus.

So we are ambassadors for Christ, since God is making his appeal through us; we entreat you on behalf of Christ, be reconciled to God.

2 Corinthians 5:20

9

New Mission

With our new beginning in Christ comes a new purpose. Paul puts it well when he says, "This one thing I do: forgetting what lies behind and straining forward to what lies ahead, I press on toward the goal for the prize of the heavenly call of God in Christ Jesus" (Philippians 3:13-14). His life is about the call of God *now*. Everything about his life is related to that one primary relationship with God. That is why he says he does "one thing." His life has come to be about God and God's will.

We might describe the "old life" as one oriented to various relationships, family, career, and even survival. If we could name one thing that was the common denominator of our various pursuits in this old way of living, it might be that we simply wanted to be happy. In the new life that is ours in Christ, however, we are realizing that happiness is not something to pursue, but a byproduct of our pursuit of the "heavenly call of God in Christ Jesus." We realize now that our mission and purpose in life comes from God.

We share in this mission with others who make up the "household of God." We may bring different gifts and forms of service to this mission, but we share the common mission of being witnesses. The risen Jesus declares to us: "You will receive power when the Holy Spirit has come upon you; and you will be my witnesses in Jerusalem, in all Judea and Samaria, and to the ends of the earth" (Acts 1:8).

What we have come to know in Christ has to be shared. As with any good news, we have to tell others. We cannot keep it to ourselves. The first thing we generally share is what God has done in our lives. We relate our experience of being brought out of the old into the new. We express our gratitude for what God has done, at first with those closest to us and then with others. We are on a mission.

As with everything else about this new life, we grow into this mission. The various elements of it become clearer as we live it. At first, it is a very personal story—our story, and then, as we become more aware of the experiences of others as well as the first Christians in the New Testament, we share more generally the narrative and the teaching of what God has done for all in Christ Jesus. We gain theological reflection and get better at articulating the message.

We become witnesses to the gospel message. We are, "ambassadors of reconciliation," bringing the message that God has come to us in Christ to bring the world back to himself (2 Corinthians 5:18-20). We proclaim the good news of a relationship with God that is for all. We let others know that it is a gift to be received.

We are witnesses by the word of our mouth and by our actions. We are sent out to love others in word and deed. We have become a "people for others." We witness by serving. We witness by the way we live.

We witness in every area of our lives. Since we belong to a community of people for others, we notice that witness takes many forms and moves out into different arenas as others in the community use their particular gifts in witness to others. Christian witness takes place in work places, among neighbors, in social institutions, in various professions, in politics and in the debates of our age.

Our witness involves "speaking the truth in love" (Ephesians 4:15). We bear witness to what is on the heart of our Father in heaven for the human family. We witness to what is right and just. We call for justice, and we do justice. In a world of evil and oppression, we are to shine as lights in the darkness—we who follow the light of the world.

The risen Jesus gave us our commission: "Go therefore and make disciples of all nations, baptizing them in the name of the Father and of the Son and of the Holy Spirit, and teaching them to obey everything that I have commanded you. And remember, I am with you always, to the end of the age." (Matthew 28:19-20)

We are under call to go out to others. We cannot simply wait for them to come to us. We are to go and make disciples. We are not only to invite others to Christ, but we must help them with their journey. We are to be trained in following Jesus and must train others. We must encourage others to keep taking steps. We help them to know about the various pitfalls and how to escape the traps and how to identify the crossroads and, above all, how to keep following Jesus no matter what happens.

Therefore, we must teach them to obey everything that Jesus has commanded. We must live a life of obedience and instruct others to do the same. There is no turning back. The new life and eternal life is ahead. We must keep following and help each other on the journey.

The good news, for followers who are witnesses, is that Jesus has promised to be with them "always, to the end of the age" (Matthew 28:20). We are assured of his help and guidance and abiding presence. "We can do all things through him who strengthens us" (Philippians 4:13). He will see us through. What he has started in us, he will bring to completion. Thanks be to God!